From The Boundary's Edge

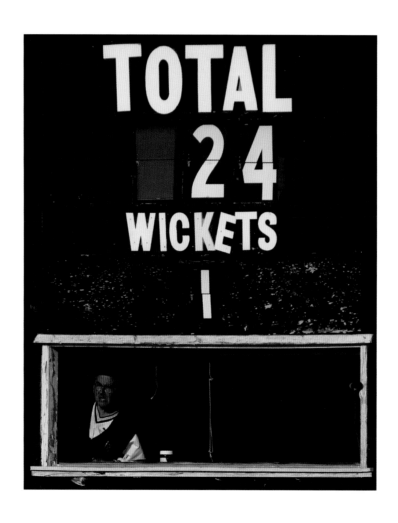

From The Boundary's Edge

Laurence Griffiths

ATLANTIC PUBLISHING

Foreword by

David Lloyd

Laurence has demonstrated yet again why he is pre-eminent among sports photographers. Swapping the big-name venues for the amateur backwaters, he shows that the great cricketing tradition is flourishing throughout the land – and the pictures themselves make you want to get out and turn your arm or wield the willow.

He gets us into the thick of the action: bowlers in delivery stride, a slip cordon waiting to pounce, batsmen in full flow, diving fielders, handsome drives, quick singles. But cricket is a game that can't be rushed. There's the change of ends, field alterations, fall of wickets – the hunt for a lost ball! Between the flurries of activity there's plenty of time to reflect, drink in the atmosphere, let the eye wander. Laurence captures the languorous indulgence, enjoyed by players and spectators alike, that cricket uniquely allows.

Sometimes it's the players, umpires, tea ladies and observers who take centre stage. And sometimes it's the stage itself that is the central delight, as in the case of Stoneleigh CC in Warwickshire, Bridgetown CC in Somerset and Hawarden Park CC in Flintshire, all recognised by *Wisden* for the beauty of their settings in which to play the most elegant of games. I particularly like the juxtaposed pictures of two encounters being played against the stunning backdrop of Bamburgh Castle in Northumberland, one a club match in whites, the other a beach knockabout. It isn't proximity that unites them, it's the love of the game. Indeed, that shines through the entire collection, which underlines cricket's status as the essence of Englishness and bucolic idyll.

From The Boundary's Edge is not only a visual feast, it is a sensory smorgasbord, conjuring up the sights, sounds and smells of a British summer. Laurence has proved – if proof were needed – that you don't need Old Father Time or superstar pros in the frame to capture the unique essence of a game that lifts the spirit and touches the soul; and that in a fast-paced, ever-changing world, cricket is a cultural anchor, comfort and joy. This magnificent volume is a glorious celebration of cricket, captured in all its majesty by the expert eye of one who shares my abiding passion for the king of games.

Newtown Linford CC, Leicestershire

Hawarden Park CC, Flintshire

Sheepscombe CC, Gloucestershire

Ambleside CC, Cumbria

Above: Castle Ashby CC, Northamptonshire
Right: Mytholmroyd CC, West Yorkshire

Booth CC, West Yorkshire

Car Colston CC, Nottinghamshire

Wormsley CC, Buckinghamshire

Keswick CC, Cumbria

Thurgarton CC, Nottinghamshire

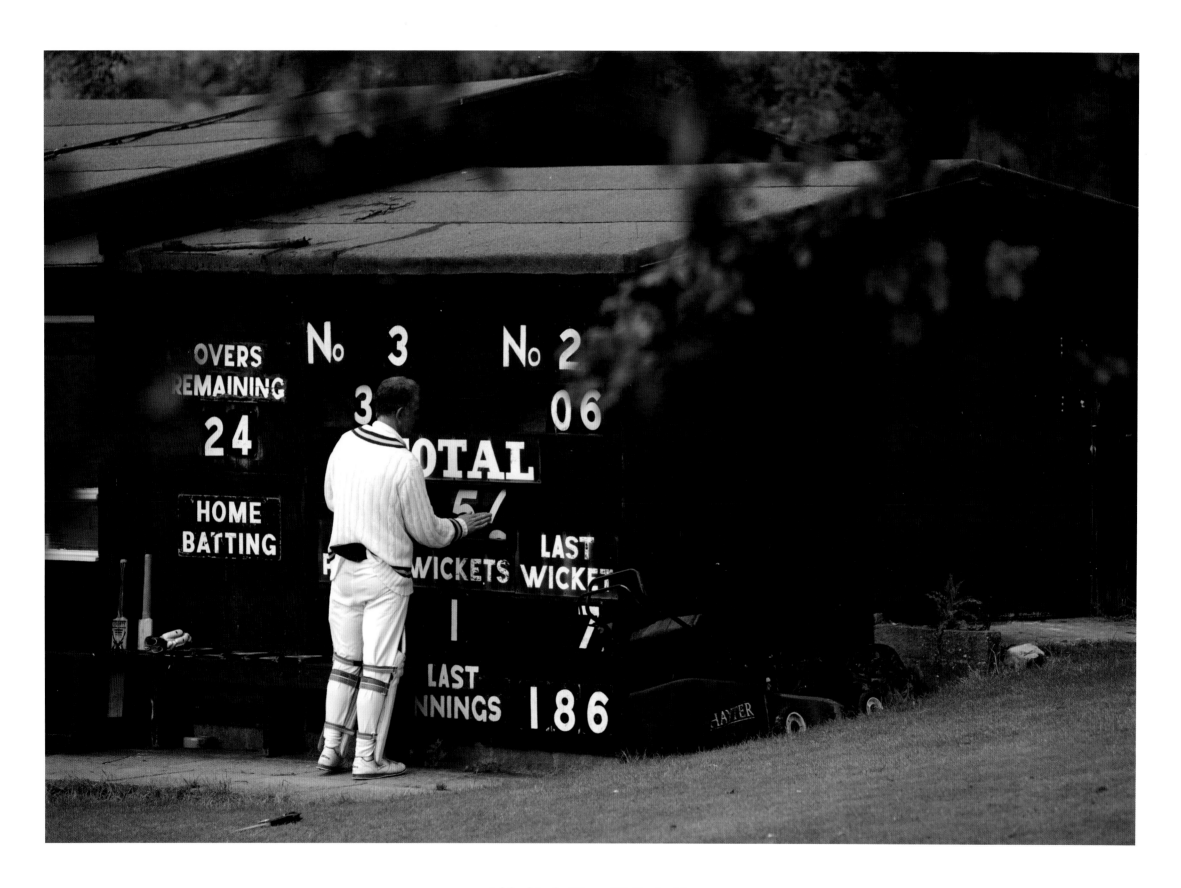

Ashford in the Water CC, Derbyshire

Sowerby Bridge CC, West Yorkshire

Marchwiel and Wrexham CC, Flintshire

Left and above: Lynton & Lynmouth CC, North Devon

Saltaire CC, Yorkshire

Booth CC, West Yorkshire

Above: Linton Park CC, Kent
Right: Stoneleigh CC, Warwickshire

Above: Ashford in the Water CC, Derbyshire
Right: Sheepscombe CC, Gloucestershire

Above and right: Wormsley CC, Buckinghamshire

Raby Castle CC, County Durham

Shipley Providence CC, Bradford

Left and above: Stoneleigh CC, Warwickshire

Above and opposite: Castle Ashby CC, Northamptonshire

Stoneleigh CC, Warwickshire

Marchwiel and Wrexham CC, Flintshire

Above: Bradfield CC, South Yorkshire
Right: Belvoir CC, Leicestershire

Left: Stoneleigh CC, Warwickshire
Above: Nottinghamshire CCC

41

Hawarden Park CC, Flintshire

Stoneleigh CC, Warwickshire

Above: Linton Park CC, Kent
Right: Leicestershire CCC

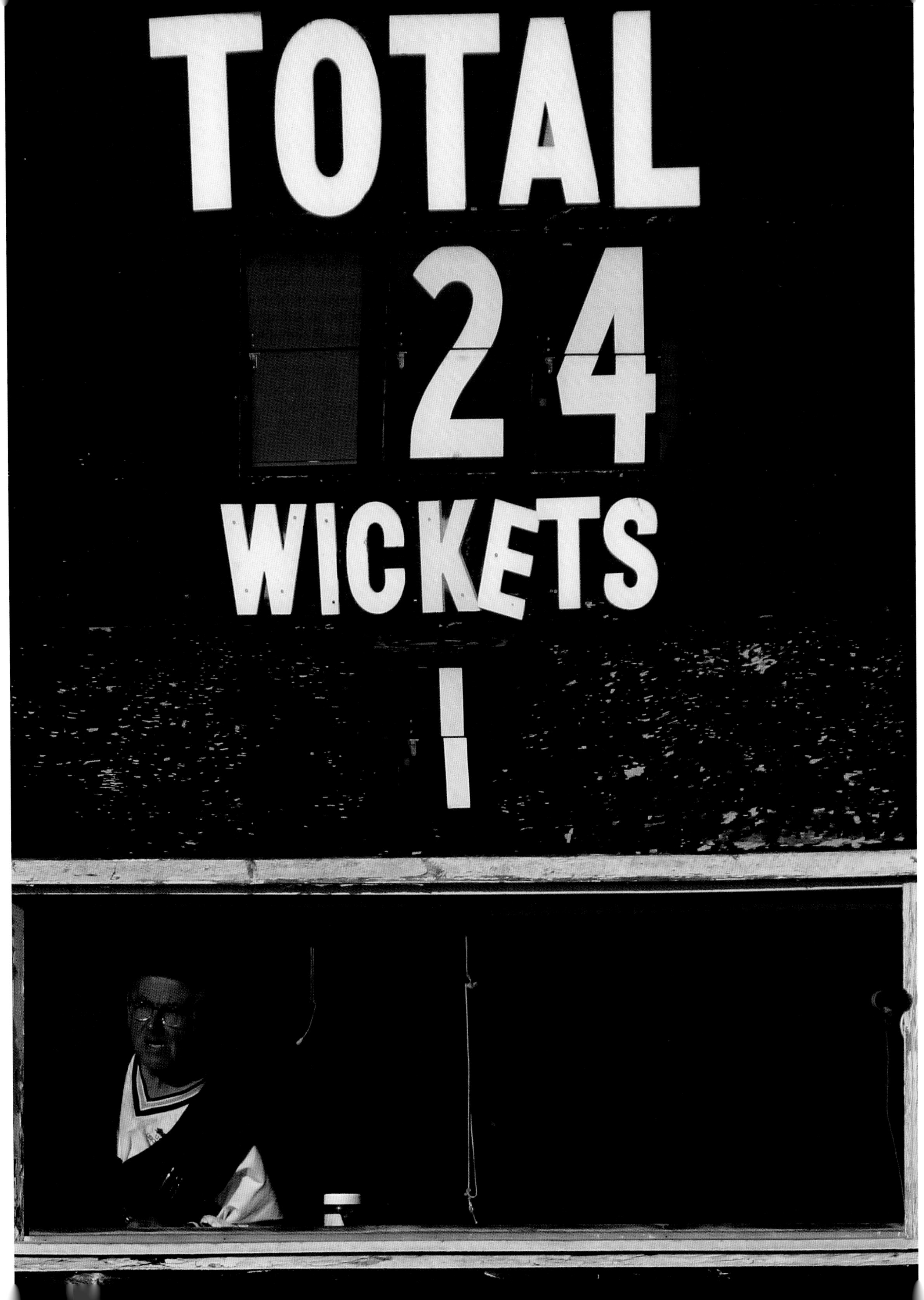
TOTAL
24
WICKETS
1

Marchwiel and Wrexham CC, Flintshire

Bradfield CC, South Yorkshire

Belvoir CC, Leicestershire

Sproxton CC, Leicestershire

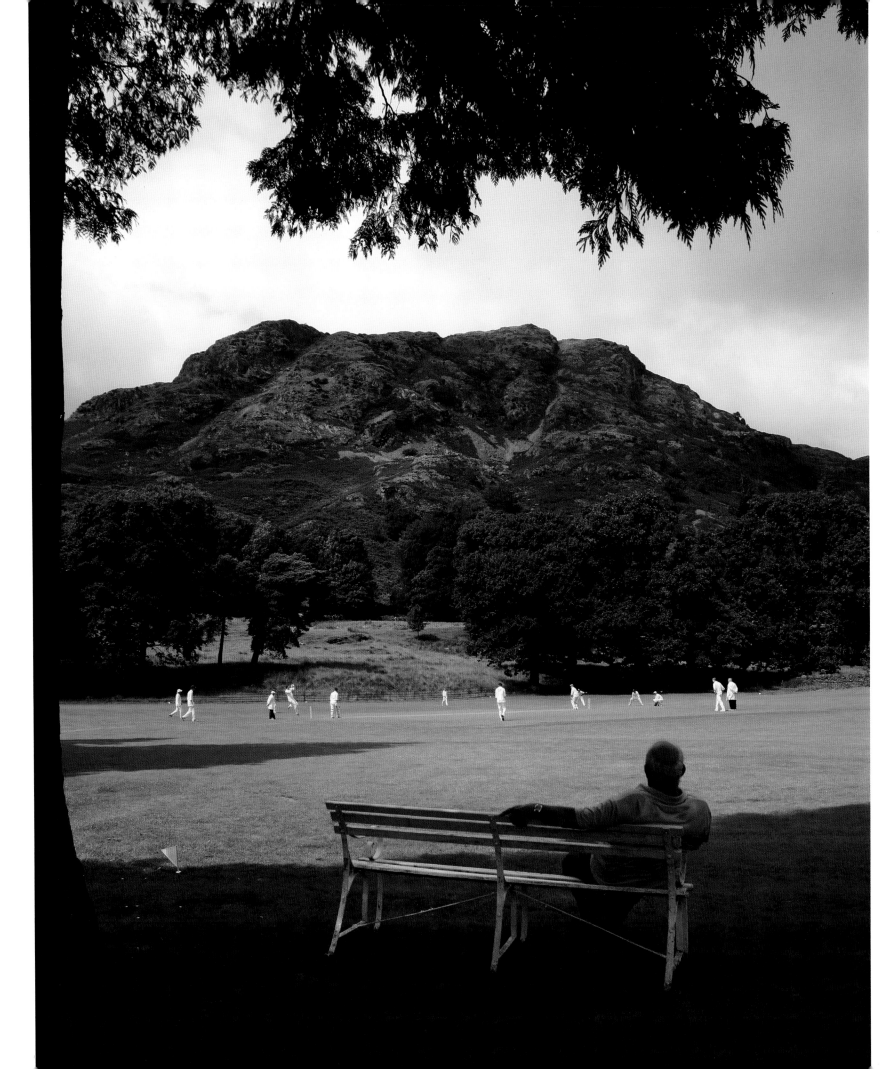

Left and right: Coniston CC, Cumbria

Booth CC, Yorkshire

Sproxton CC, Leicestershire

Above: Stoneleigh CC, Warwickshire
Right: Ashford in the Water CC, Derbyshire

Stoneleigh CC, Warwickshire

Rastrick CC, West Yorkshire

Left and above: Castle Ashby CC, Northamptonshire

Sheepscombe CC, Gloucestershire

Belvoir CC, Leicestershire

Bamburgh Beach, Northumberland

South Sands Beach, Devon

Left: Raby Castle CC, County Durham
Above: Wormsley CC, Buckinghamshire

Belvoir CC, Leicestershire

Warsop Stebbing bats, handcrafted in East Hanningfield, Essex

Booth CC, West Yorkshire

Above: Bradfield CC, South Yorkshire
Overleaf: Castle Ashby CC, Northamptonshire

Bamburgh Castle CC, Northumberland

Coniston CC, Cumbria

Bridgetown CC, West Somerset

Bridgetown CC, West Somerset

Above, right and overleaf: The Ship Inn CC, Fife, Scotland

Booth CC, West Yorkshire

Ranby House School, Nottinghamshire

Left: Lynton & Lynmouth Cricket Club, North Devon
Above: Stoneleigh CC, Warwickshire

Sheepscombe CC, Gloucestershire

Bradfield CC, South Yorkshire

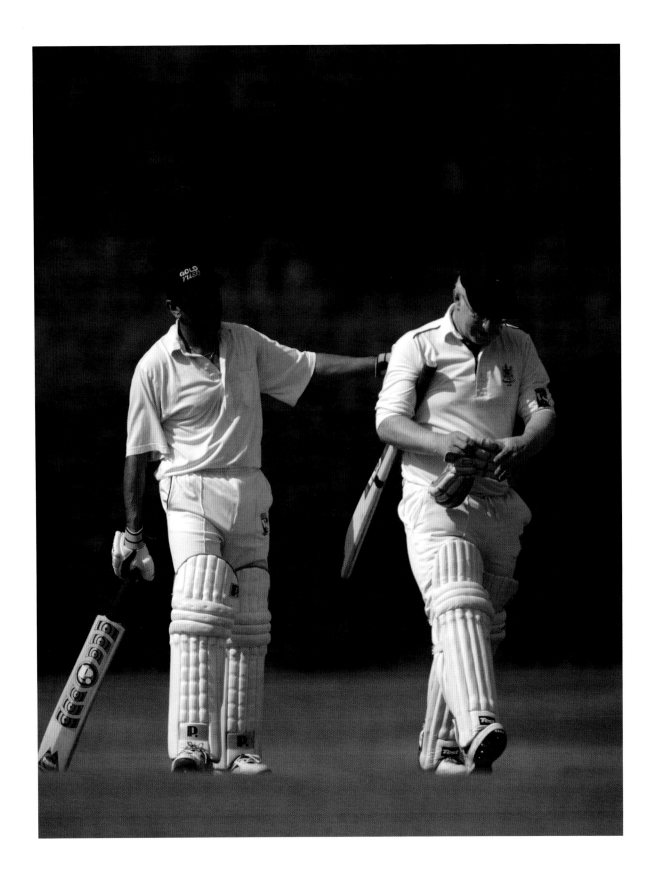

Above: Stoneleigh CC, Warwickshire
Left: The Old Pavilion, Castle Ashby CC, Northamptonshire

Thurgarton CC, Nottinghamshire

Booth CC, West Yorkshire

Bamburgh CC, Northumberland

Bamburgh Beach, Northumberland

Above: Belvoir CC, Leicestershire
Right: Monkton Combe CC, Somerset

TOTAL 89
WKTS 9
OVERS 2
LAST 100
INNS

Above: Bradfield CC, South Yorkshire
Right: Monkton Combe CC, Somerset

In loving memory of Keith Selby

This book is dedicated to my beautiful wife, Rachael and my wonderful children Isaac, Louie and Esme.

Published by Atlantic Publishing

First published in 2011

Atlantic Publishing
38 Copthorne Road, Croxley Green, Hertfordshire WD3 4AQ, UK

© Atlantic Publishing

All images © Getty Images

Special thanks must go to Graham Chadwick for making cricket and life fun, Rick Mayston for never giving up on this book,
Adrian Murrell, Steve Rose and Nick Evans-Lombe at Getty Images, Greg and Christine at Atlantic for having faith in this project
and all the wonderful people at all the clubs I have visited.

Thanks also to Rob Marsh, Pat Murphy, Stephen Brenkley, David Lloyd, Phil Tufnell, Graham Swann, Mark Butcher, Michael Vaughan, Andrew Flintoff,
Darren Gough, Alec Stewart, Michael Regan, David Munden, Patrick Eager, Shaun Botterill, Ben Radford, David Pillinger, Kenny Roger, Clive Mason,
Stu Forster for his fairness, Phil Brown, Dickie Pelham, Eddie Keogh, Andy Hooper, Richard Moore, Drew Shannon, David Ashdown, Dave Jones,
Gareth Copley, Frank Baron, Ross Kinnaird, Steve Etherington, Phil O'Brien, Neal Simpson, Bernard Poole, Andy Afford, Phillip Brown, Colin Panter,
Lynne, Giles, Mark, Helene, Mum, Dad, Dave, Jean, Louise and Billy, Oliver.

A catalogue record for this book is available from the British Library.

ISBN 978-0-9557949-7-1

Printed in China